WEEKLY WR READER®
EARLY LEARNING LIBRARY

Great Americans
Thomas Jefferson

Monica L. Rausch

Reading consultant: Susan Nations, M.Ed., author/literacy coach/
consultant in literacy development

Chapter 1

Jefferson: Author, Farmer, President

In June 1776, Thomas Jefferson was hard at work, writing and writing and writing. The leaders of the American **colonies** were waiting to see what he wrote.

On June 28, Jefferson showed his work to the leaders. It expressed their ideas perfectly! On July 4, 1776, they approved his document. It said that the American colonies were free of British rule. The leaders called it their **Declaration of Independence**!

Jefferson was not only a writer. • He was also a lawyer, a farmer, an **architect**, and an **inventor**. • He was the third president of the United States, too!

Benjamin Franklin (*left*) and John Adams (*center*) talked to Thomas Jefferson about the Declaration of Independence. His first drafts of the declaration cover the floor.

The Jefferson plantation was huge. Streams and fields divided it into separate farms and areas, including the vegetable garden shown here.

Jefferson was born on April 13, 1743, in Virginia. His family lived on a big farm, called a **plantation**.

Jefferson was tall and thin with sandy hair and freckles. He was shy, but he was a good student. Jefferson loved learning. He studied math and science. He also learned about the land on his father's farm.

When Jefferson was fourteen, his father died. Three years later, he went to college, and then he studied law. When Jefferson turned twenty-one, he became the owner of the farm. Soon, Jefferson also started working as a lawyer.

Jefferson attended the College of William and Mary in Williamsburg, Virginia, during the early 1760s.

© North Wind Picture Archives

© North Wind Picture Archives

Jefferson still liked to run the farm. He tried planting many different kinds of fruits and vegetables. He wrote down the names of all the plants growing there.

Jefferson had **slaves** on his farm. They worked in the fields and in his house.

Slaves, like this one, worked in plantation homes. They were often better dressed than field slaves. Jefferson owned about 150 slaves.

Jefferson also liked to draw plans for buildings. In 1769, he drew plans for a new home. He started building this big house on a small hill. He called the house "Monticello." *Monticello* means "little mountain."

Three years later, Jefferson married Martha Wayles Skelton. Thomas and Martha Jefferson had six children. Only two children lived to be adults.

Jefferson added more rooms to Monticello in 1796. It now has forty-three rooms.

© North Wind Picture Archives

Chapter 2

Freeing the Colonies

Jefferson began to work for the Virginia government in 1769. Virginia was a British colony. In 1774, Great Britain made laws that the people of Virginia did not like.

Other colonies also opposed the laws. Virginia and the other colonies decided not to follow these laws. The British king ordered them to obey. In April 1775, the British army and people in the colonies started to fight. The **American Revolution** had begun!

In 1776, leaders from all the colonies met, including Jefferson. They talked about freeing the colonies from British rule. They wanted to make their own laws. Jefferson wrote down their ideas, creating the Declaration of Independence.

In 1776, the colony leaders met in this room in Independence Hall in Philadelphia, Pennsylvania.

Jefferson drew the plans for the Virginia State Capitol building in 1784.

After the meeting, Jefferson went back to Virginia. He became the **governor** of Virginia in 1779. While he was governor, the British army came to Virginia to catch him. He barely escaped!

After being governor for three years, Jefferson wanted to rest. He did not like speaking in public, but he did like to write. In 1781, he went home to Monticello and wrote a book about the plants, animals, and people of Virginia.

In 1782, Jefferson's wife died. Jefferson was very sad. He did not want to leave Monticello, but his friend, George Washington, wanted his help. Jefferson decided to work for the government again. In 1784, he became a **diplomat** and went to France.

When Jefferson traveled to France, he took his teenage daughter, Martha, with him. She is shown here as a young woman.

© North Wind Picture Archives

Chapter 3

The Presidency

George Washington became president in 1789. He asked Jefferson to be part of his **cabinet**. He also asked Alexander Hamilton to be in his cabinet.

Hamilton and Jefferson soon began to argue. Jefferson believed the government should not have a lot of power. He thought the government should make only a few laws. Hamilton thought the government should have more power. Jefferson left the government in 1793.

In 1796, Jefferson ran for president but lost. He became vice president. In 1800, Jefferson ran for president again. This time he won!

While Washington was president, Alexander Hamilton was in charge of the United States' money. Here, he stands between Henry Knox (*left*) and Jefferson (*right*).

The USS *Constitution (left)* fights pirates at Tripoli, part of today's Lebanon, in the Mediterranean Sea.

Jefferson did many important things while president. He helped American ships that were being attacked by pirates. He sent the navy to fight the pirates.

Jefferson wanted the United States to grow. He bought a large piece of land from France. This land was west of the Mississippi River. The United States was now twice as big as before!

The land Jefferson bought was called the Louisiana Purchase. This area is colored orange on this map.

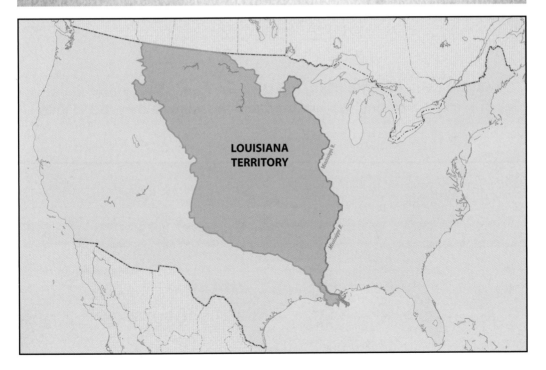

President Jefferson wanted to know more about the land he bought. He sent two men, Meriwether Lewis and William Clark, to explore the land. The men reported back to Jefferson.

In 1804, Jefferson ran for president again. Many people liked him as president, and he easily won the election.

Lewis and Clark traveled along the Missouri River. They wrote many reports about the land they explored and the animals they found there.

© North Wind Picture Archives

Chapter 4

Retirement

In 1809, Jefferson's time as president ended. He went back to Monticello. Jefferson wanted to help people learn. He made plans for a new college, found teachers, and started the University of Virginia.

Jefferson also spent time reading, writing, and collecting books. In 1815, after the national library burned down, Jefferson sold sixty-seven hundred books to the U.S. government. The books helped start a new national library.

Jefferson helped make a machine that copied a letter. The machine connected two pens. When a person wrote a letter with one pen, the other pen would write the letter, too.

Jefferson had lots of ideas. He liked to find ways to save time and save space. Jefferson found a way to make the plow better. He also developed a way to make better copies of letters. Jefferson designed a book holder. It can keep five books open at once!

Jefferson wrote many letters to his friend John Adams and to his grandchildren. The grandchildren visited Jefferson. He liked to play games with them.

In July 1826, Jefferson became sick. He died on July 4, 1826. Many landmarks named in honor of this great writer, thinker, and president now dot the nation he helped form.

Thomas Jefferson is honored as one of four presidents whose faces are carved into Mount Rushmore. Jefferson is between George Washington *(far left)* and Theodore Roosevelt *(second from right)*. Abraham Lincoln is also carved into the mountain.

Glossary

American Revolution — the war fought between the American colonies and Great Britain, which ruled them. The colonies won the war and became free of British control.

architect — a person who draws plans for, or designs, buildings

cabinet — a group of people who work for the president and help him make decisions

colonies — lands and people ruled by another country

Declaration of Independence — the statement made by the American colonies telling Great Britain that the colonies were free

designed — thought up and made a plan for

diplomat — a person who speaks about his or her country to leaders of another country

document — a piece of writing that gives information

governor — a person who governs, or rules, a colony or state

inventor — someone who creates or designs an object for the first time

landmarks — important buildings or artworks

plantation — a large area of land that is farmed

plow — a tool used to break up the soil to prepare it for planting

slaves — people treated as property and forced to work without pay

For More Information vw review

Books

Meet Thomas Jefferson. Landmark Books (series). Marvin Barrett (Random House)

Meet Thomas Jefferson. Patricia Pingry (Ideals Children's Books)

A Picture Book of Thomas Jefferson. Picture Book Biography (series). James Cross Giblin (Scholastic Paperbacks)

Thomas Jefferson: Third President 1801-1809. Getting to Know the U.S. Presidents (series). Mike Venezia (Children's Press)

Web Sites

American President: Thomas Jefferson
www.americanpresident.org/history/thomasjefferson
A short biography of Thomas Jefferson

Jump Back in Time: Thomas Jefferson
www.americaslibrary.gov/cgi-bin/page.cgi/jb/colonial/jefferso_1
Learn about Jefferson's achievements

Index

About the Author

Monica L. Rausch has a master's degree in creative writing from the University of Wisconsin-Milwaukee, where she is currently teaching composition, literature, and creative writing. She likes to write fiction, but sticking to the facts is fun, too. Monica lives in Milwaukee near her six nieces and nephews, to whom she loves to read books.